THE FLAT TAX
FREEDOM, FAIRNESS, JOBS, and GROWTH

Daniel Mitchell,
The Heritage Foundation

REGNERY PUBLISHING, INC.
WASHINGTON, D.C.

Library of Congress Cataloging-in-Publication Data

Mitchell, Daniel J., 1958–
The Flat Tax: freedom, fairness, jobs, and growth / by Daniel J. Mitchell.
    p.   cm.
    ISBN 0-89526-709-8
    1. Flat-rate income tax—United States.   2. Income Tax—United
    States. I. Title.
    HJ4652.M547   1996
    336.24'2—dc20   96-10994
                                  CIP

Published in the United States of America by
REGNERY PUBLISHING, INC.
An Eagle Publishing Company

422 First Street, SE
Washington, DC 20003

Design by Marja Walker

Distributed to the trade by
National Book Network
4720-A Boston Way
Lanham, MD 20706

10 9 8 7 6 5 4 3 2 1

Books are available in quantity for promotional or premium use. Write to Director of Special Sales, Regnery Publishing, Inc., 422 First Street, SE Washington, DC 20003, for information on discounts and terms or call (202) 546-5005.

TABLE OF CONTENTS

PREFACE BY JACK KEMP

In the heat of a political campaign, ideas get tossed around rather freely. Often times, in the rancor of debate, good policies get shunted aside while others less worthy of consideration seem to gain support.

However, in the current presidential political season, no idea has generated more enthusiasm or support than that of a flatter, fairer, and simpler tax code for America. At the same time, however, no idea has come under more attack from both journalists and politicians on the left.

I believe that the benefits of a simple, flat tax rate system are so overwhelming that its fate deserves to be decided on its merits—not by a few sound bites on the evening news or in articles written by economists wedded to the tax-and-spend policies of the past. That's why my friend Daniel J. Mitchell, the McKenna Senior Fellow in Political Economy at The Heritage Foundation, has written *The Flat Tax: Freedom, Fairness, Jobs, and Growth*.

Dan Mitchell uses plain English and common-sense economics to correct the inaccuracies being bandied about by the special interests. He makes a principled case for the flat-tax "cause" and shows why it is superior to other tax-reform proposals. And Dan lets you see for yourself if you would benefit from a single rate system by allowing you to compare your current federal tax bill to what your tax bill would be under the flat tax's simple calculation.

Most importantly, *The Flat Tax: Freedom, Fairness, Jobs, and Growth* reveals how the flat tax could be America's ticket to unparalleled growth and opportunity in the next century. After our victory in the Cold War, America stands at the edge of a new millennium with untold possibilities. We are poised to lead the world into a new era of prosperity. But to confront this daunting challenge foursquare, we must free ourselves of barriers to growth and opportunity.

So far, one overwhelming lesson has emerged from the 1996 presidential selection process: voters are worried about America's capacity to face that economic challenge. Some have suggested that America should avoid this challenge—that we should pursue a policy of "economic nationalism" by raising tariffs on imports. I reject this big-government, protectionist solution to the problems of working Americans. The enemy of America is not Mexico or Asia; our enemies are the policies in Washington, D.C., that make our country less competitive. And there is no greater impediment to America's future than our current federal income tax code.

Dan Mitchell minces no words. He frankly states that "our tax system is a disgrace." He explains how our tax code has been turned from a simple tool to raise revenue for government into a complicated instrument with an impossible aim: to redistribute wealth. As a result, the seven-million-word Internal Revenue Code is impossibly complex, economically destructive, and manifestly unfair. Our nation's capital has become occupied by armies of accountants, tax specialists, and lobbyists seeking to curry favor in exchange for loopholes and deductions.

Escalating marginal tax rates and advancing IRS intrusiveness have created a federal tax system that is beyond repair. The link between effort and reward has been broken; productivity has declined and jobs have left our shores. Wildly excessive and unjust taxes have locked away access to capital and credit needed to increase the real output, productivity, and wages of the working men and women of America.

Our entrepreneurial spirit, built on dynamism and hope, is increasingly threatened by what House Majority Leader Dick Armey (R-Tex.) has called the "Clinton Crunch"—an economic squeeze between falling wages and rising taxes. Not only do Americans earn less, but, thanks to the federal tax policies, they take home less of what they earn.

Sensing that we need a new tax system that reflects our highest values and unleashes our greatest potential, Senate Majority Leader Bob Dole and House Speaker Newt Gingrich appointed me to chair the National Commission on Economic Growth and Tax Reform. Our job was to study the current tax code, to listen to suggestions from around the country, and to offer a design for an entirely new tax system for America's 21st century.

We operated under the premise than an economic growth rate of 2.4%—currently considered "optimistic" by the Congressional Budget Office and the Office of Management and Budget—is unacceptable to the American people. The commission sought to frame a new tax system that would promise a booming economy, promote job creation, and ensure the greatest possible opportunity for all Americans to work, save, invest, and reach their potential.

We took our bearings from these words of President Kennedy, which served as an inspiration for me in the early 1980s when the tax-reform movement was launched with the Kemp/Roth tax cut:

> Tax rates are too high today and tax revenues are too low, and
> the soundest way to raise the revenues in the long run is to cut
> the rates now… to achieve the more prosperous, expanding
> economy which can bring a budget surplus.

These words are as true today as they were in December 1962

when John F. Kennedy spoke before the Economic Club of New York—a fact that Dan Mitchell makes clear.

Heeding this wisdom, in our report, *Unleashing America's Potential*, the tax-reform commission established principles to guide us to our vision of a new tax code:

- The tax code must be simple and fair.
- It must generate sufficient revenue for the legitimate tasks of government.
- It must not place a tax burden on those least able to bear one.
- It must not restrict the creativity and hard work of Americans to raise living standards and our general prosperity.

In this book, Dan Mitchell shows that a flat tax would best exemplify many of the principles sought by our commission: a single, low tax rate with a generous personal exemption; a lower tax burden on America's working families and those least able to pay; ending biases against work, saving, and investment; allowing full deductibility of the payroll tax for working men and women; squeezing out the influence of lobbyists by requiring a two-thirds supermajority in Congress to increase tax rates.

Only a pro-growth tax code can restore America's confidence at home and her greatness abroad. We need to liberate the American dream and remove the barriers to upward social and economic mobility. The American ethos of entrepreneurship and optimism made America great. Dan Mitchell is right: the flat tax will bolster that ethos and help restore integrity and honesty to Washington.

INTRODUCTION BY
SENATOR RICHARD SHELBY

The current federal tax system is unfair, overly complicated, and punishes individuals who work hard, save, and invest. This is why House Majority Leader Dick Armey and I introduced the "Freedom and Fairness Restoration Act," also know as the Armey-Shelby flat tax, in July of 1995.

From the individual trying to start a new business to the parents trying to put food on the table for their children or seniors living off the savings of a lifetime, the current income tax system restrains individual freedom and obstructs economic opportunity. In contrast, the flat tax is specifically designed to promote freedom, fairness, and economic opportunity, in several ways. First, the flat tax lowers the marginal tax rates, thereby lifting the disincentives to work the extra hour. Many times individuals work hard on Saturday and Sunday in hopes of receiving overtime pay, only to see the fruits of their additional labor taken away by the government. Under the flat tax, a dollar is a dollar. The flat tax will not punish you for going the extra mile, working the extra hour, or making the extra dollar. Just because you work harder does not mean the government should take more.

In addition, the flat tax takes politics out of the tax code. In exchange for drastically lowering tax rates, it eliminates *all* loopholes, *all* government coercion, and *all* sweetheart tax deals for special interests. As Daniel Mitchell illustrates so effectively in this book, most of the special interest lobbying that occurs in

Washington is over attempts to secure special favors in the tax code. Pass the flat tax and many special interests will close their doors the next day.

The flat tax also encourages economic freedom by allowing generous family allowances. The Armey-Shelby flat tax has a family allowance of $33,300 for a family of four. Majority Leader Armey and I believe the family should be able to keep that money to feed the children, put a roof over their heads, and generally take care of the family. You earned it, you should keep it. Such a generous allowance would take millions of lower income families off the tax roll and help others provide for their families.

Fairness is also a central issue of the flat tax. To be fair means to be marked by impartiality and honesty; free from self-interest, prejudice, or favoritism. Under a flat tax, everyone is given a personal allowance and everyone with children is given an allowance for their children. Most importantly, everyone pays the same flat percentage of taxes on each dollar above the allowance.

In the case of the Armey-Shelby flat tax, a family of four earning $33,300 would pay no federal tax. The same family earning $55,000 would pay $2,839, or 6 percent, and the family earning $100,00 would pay $11,339, or 11 percent. The personal allowance causes the *effective* rate to be progressive… a fact most people consider fair.

The flat tax also goes a long way in promoting economic opportunity. While the current tax code punishes individuals who save and invest, the flat tax repeals the double taxation of investment income by taxing it once and only once at the source. As a result, individuals will not feel that their savings are "locked-in" and will be able to move their investments to the highest valued use.

The elimination of double and even triple taxation removes the hindrance to capital formation. That will increase productivity.

Savings permits employers and employees to invest in the tools and capital equipment necessary to increase production, and that raises wages. Eliminating the double and triple taxation is the most effective action Congress can take to increase the economic opportunity for the average worker.

As this book will explain, the flat tax will lower interest rates by about 25 percent. For the individual, lower interest rates will help lower home mortgage interest payments, car payments, and even school loans. For businesses, lower interest rates will reduce the costs of capital equipment, again aiding the business in increasing the productivity of the workers and ultimately their wages.

Skeptics of the flat tax argue against the removal of home mortgage interest and/or the charitable deductions. In the current onerous tax code, I would agree with them. However, these deductions are not necessary in a flat-tax world. People do not buy homes just to take advantage of the home mortgage interest deduction. Rather, individuals buy homes to invest in the future and for the security and stability of home ownership. People do not donate to charity just to take the deduction, but because they really believe in the cause of the particular charity. As you will see, relatively few people take these deductions—the vast majority do not.

The flat tax is about growth and opportunity. All economists agree the flat tax would increase growth in the economy. The debate centers around how much. In these times of sluggish growth and stagnant wages, the flat tax is the solution. The flat tax would help families put food on the table, help small businesses get the capital they need and increase the wages of American workers. In short, the flat tax would provide an environment for unprecedented economic growth from which everyone would benefit.

CHAPTER 1
WHAT IS A FLAT TAX?

Our tax system is a disgrace. It is a complicated failure that hinders the nation's growth while giving special breaks to the politically well-connected. The tax code's biggest victims are middle-class taxpayers. Average citizens can't afford to hire high-priced lawyers and accountants to navigate the incomprehensible rules and regulations promulgated by the IRS. And yet, however bewildered normal taxpayers may be in the face of the tax code's complexity, they are held accountable for the slightest mistake on their tax forms—even if it is the result of IRS advice!

Tax law has become so complex that half of all Americans now need professional tax preparers to fill out their returns. Tax preparation and compliance costs the economy about $140 billion per year, an average of more than $1,000 for every taxpayer. Most of this is paid by business, and passed along as higher prices and lower wages.

Not only are taxes too complex, they are too high. After World War II, the average family sent only about 3 percent of its income to Washington. The same family today coughs up 24 percent of its earnings to the federal tax collector, and the situation is getting worse with each passing year. Once state and local taxes are added to the federal take, taxes make up the biggest slice of the average family's budget, exceeding the *combined* total spent on food, clothing, shelter, and transportation. (See Chart 1.) The relentless encroachment of taxation is the main reason that for many families one breadwinner is no longer enough.

CHART 1

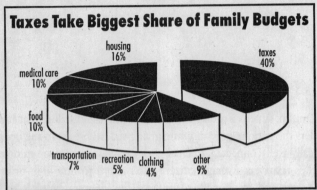

Taxes Take Biggest Share of Family Budgets

housing 16%

taxes 40%

medical care 10%

food 10%

transportation 7%

recreation 5%

clothing 4%

other 9%

Today's tax system is not only unbearably complex and ultimately ruinous, worst of all it punishes us for doing what is right.

- If you work hard or even take a second job, you might think your sacrifice would be rewarded. Not by the government: Working harder and trying to get ahead simply bumps you into a higher tax bracket.

- If you have any money left over after paying for taxes and necessities, you might think the government would reward you for saving. Just the opposite: Build a nest egg and the government taxes that income a second time when it earns interest.

- Investing in America's economic future is something the government should encourage, right? Well, the joke's on you. If your investment pays off, the government grabs a big portion through corporate income taxes, capital gains taxes, and personal income taxes. Needless to say, you get stuck with the losses if the investment does not pay off.

The current tax code has turned the government into the enemy of prosperity and freedom, and has created a parasitic ruling class that takes our money and warps our values.

There is a solution. A simple and fair tax system can restore honesty to government and growth to the economy—the *flat tax*. Based on an idea developed by two economists at Stanford University's Hoover Institution, and introduced as legislation by House Majority Leader Dick Armey and Senator Richard Shelby, the flat tax has four features that make it particularly attractive to ordinary citizens.

1. *Single low rate.* All Americans would pay the same low rate of 17 percent on their *taxable* income. The baseline for taxable income would be raised, however, so that a family of four would pay no income tax on the first $33,300 of income.
2. *Simplicity.* All citizens would fill out the same postcard-sized form to pay their taxes. No more expensive experts to fill out tax returns of mind-boggling complexity.
3. *Get politics out of the tax code by elimination of deductions, credits, and exemptions.* Politicians manipulate us by using the tax code to encourage certain behaviors and discourage others. Some of these tax incentives and loopholes may seem hard to give up, but in exchange we would get lower taxes, less interference from Washington in our lives, and put many of the sleazy special interest lobbyists out of business.
4. *No double dipping.* The flat tax ends the double taxation of income saved or invested. That will help guarantee seniors better living standards, help families save for college, and mean billions more in investments and savings to build businesses, raise wages, and create jobs.

The flat tax is not just the fancy of some ivory-tower academics—it works in the real world. The one country in the world whose tax system can be called a flat tax is Hong Kong. It also happens to be the fastest growing economy in the world in the last fifty years.

Consider these basic facts about Hong Kong's economy and fiscal policy: Hong Kong's average growth rate since World War II has exceeded 7 percent, more than double the average rate of growth in the United States. The average income in Hong Kong is roughly $25,000, a figure that rivals the average income in the United States. What makes this particularly amazing is that average income in Hong Kong after World War II was less than $200. Hong Kong consistently enjoys budget surpluses and has reserves (the opposite of national debt) of $60 billion. The unemployment rate in Hong Kong has never exceeded 3 percent, even with high levels of immigration. And even though the tax rate is effectively flat, it is demonstrably fair: The wealthiest 10 percent pay about 75 percent of Hong Kong's taxes.

Our own history offers powerful evidence. The three times we have lowered tax rates and moved in the direction of a flat tax—the 1920s, the 1960s, and the 1980s—the economy boomed. Periods of rising tax rates—the 1930s, the 1970s, and the 1990s—have resulted in weaker economies. The flat tax has been put to the test and it works.

More than two centuries ago, colonists dressed as Indians threw tea into Boston Harbor to protest unjust taxes. This tax revolt helped trigger the American Revolution and led to the creation of a society based on freedom and prosperity. Ever since the income tax was enacted, however, we have been punished for working, penalized for saving, and gouged for investing.

If we want to restore freedom to America, the tax code must be repealed and replaced by a simple and fair flat tax.

CHAPTER 2
WHAT ARE THE ADVANTAGES OF A FLAT TAX?

Here are the major benefits of a flat tax:

Faster economic growth. With a low flat tax, we would get to keep more of the money we earn, a fact that would make it far more appealing to work, save, and invest. These are the productive economic behaviors that will boost the economy's long-term growth rate and ensure prosperity. Even if a flat tax lifted long-term growth by as little as 0.5 percent (and most estimates show growth increasing by twice that amount), the income of the average family of four after ten years would be as much as five thousand dollars higher than otherwise.

Instant wealth creation. When savings and investments are no longer taxed twice, they will be worth more. According to Harvard economist Dale Jorgenson, eliminating double taxation will boost national wealth by some one trillion dollars. The reason? Without taxes to eat up the interest on earnings, assets will produce more net income. An asset that produces more income is an asset that is more valuable.

Simplicity. For many Americans the most persuasive feature of a flat tax is its simplicity. According to a study conducted for the IRS, the current tax code requires taxpayers to devote 5.4 billion hours each year to their tax returns. Yet even this commitment of time is no guarantee of accuracy: The code is so complex that even tax experts and the IRS often make mistakes. Under a flat tax the complicated documents and instruction manuals taxpayers struggle

CHART 2

Form 1	Individual Wage Tax		1997

Your first name and initial (if joint return, also give spouse's name and initial)   Last name | Your social security number

Home address (number and street including apartment number or rural route) | Spouse's social security number

City, town, or post office, state and ZIP code | Your occupation

| | | Spouse's occupation

1	Wages and salary and Pensions	1	
2	Personal allowance		
	(a) $22,700 for married filing jointly	2(a)	
	(b) $11,350 for single	2(b)	
	(c) $14,850 for single head of household	2(c)	
3	Number of dependents, not including spouse	3	
4	Personal allowances for dependents(line 3 multiplied by $5,300)	4	
5	Total personal allowances(line 2 plus line 4)	5	
6	Taxable wages(line 1 less line 5, if positive: otherwise zero)	6	
7	Tax (17% of line 6)	7	
8	Tax already paid	8	
9	Tax due (line 7 less line 8, if positive)	9	
10	Refund due (line 8 less line 7, if positive)	10	

Form 2	Business Tax		1997

Business name | Employer identification number

Street address | County

City, town, or post office, state and ZIP code | Principal product

1	Gross revenue from sales	1	
2	Allowable costs		
	(a) Purchases of goods, services, and materials	2(a)	
	(b) Wages, salaries, and retirement benefits	2(b)	
	(c) Purchases of capital equipment and land	2(c)	
3	Total allowable costs(sum of lines 2(a), 2(b), and 2(c))	3	
4	Taxable income(line 1 less line 3)	4	
5	Tax (17% of line 4)	5	
6	Carry-forward from 1997	6	
7	Interest on carry-forward (6 percent of line 6)	7	
8	Carry-forward into 1998 (line 6 plus line 7)	8	
9	Tax due (line 5 less line 8, if positive)	9	
10	Carry forward to 1999 (line 8 less line 5, if positive)	10	

to decipher every April would be replaced by a brief set of instructions. The lengthy forms would be scrapped in favor of a simple postcard-sized return. (See Chart 2.) All taxpayers, from General Motors to a teenager flipping hamburgers, would be able to file their taxes using a postcard-sized form. This isn't just a matter of reducing the hassle factor: The cost we all pay in lost time and expensive tax preparation in order to comply with the tax code would drop by tens of billions of dollars.

Increased civil liberties. When the tax code is complex, there is more room for abuse and tax evasion. As the tax code has grown in complexity the enforcement power of the IRS has grown too. But the IRS's quest to quash abuse and evasion has meant innumerable kafkaesque trials for decent taxpayers suspected of violating one or another provision of the tax code. Under current law, murder defendants have more rights than IRS-targeted taxpayers. With a simpler, fairer tax code, there would just be less for the IRS to do. The only possible questions the IRS could ask are: What is your income? How big is your family? Infringements on freedom and privacy would fall dramatically.

Fairness. A flat tax would treat people equally. If Mr. Smith had one thousand times the taxable income of Mr. Jones, he would pay one thousand times more in taxes than Mr. Jones. Nor would Mr. Smith be able to avoid paying his share by using elaborate tax shelters and fancy loopholes. Average taxpayers would lose the nagging fear that by paying their taxes they are being suckered.

An end to political favoritism. The flat tax gets rid of all deductions, preferences, exclusions, loopholes, credits, and exemptions. Politicians would lose their power to pick winners and losers, to reward friends and punish enemies. Instead of making decisions on the basis of the tax code, investors and businesses would be driven by sound business reasons. Instead of investing in the careers of politicians, businesses would have more resources to invest in their employees.

CHAPTER 3
CALCULATING HOW YOU BENEFIT FROM A FLAT TAX

Using the IRS's own data, The Heritage Foundation has calculated that the average taxpayer will save more than one thousand dollars under a flat tax. The Tax Foundation has similar estimates, with average taxpayer savings of one thousand dollars under a 17 percent flat tax.

One benefit of simplicity is that taxpayers do not need to consult a tax attorney to find out how they would fare under a flat tax. Because of the easy postcard-sized form, all taxpayers can immediately tell whether, and how much, they will save on their taxes. All taxpayers need to know is the size of their family and how much they earned in the form of wages, salaries, and pensions. They do not need to worry about interest, dividends, capital gains, rents, royalties, and other business income. Taxes on those forms of income are withheld and paid at the business level.

Here are a few examples to show how the flat tax would affect different taxpayers.

Frank Jones is a twenty-year-old blue-collar worker. He is just beginning his working career, is not married, and earns $23,000 a year. He lives in an apartment and does not take itemized deductions. Having heard that the flat tax has big deductions for children, Frank figures he will be a loser. He will be pleasantly surprised. Under the current tax system, he pays $2,430. Under a 17 percent flat tax, his bill falls to $1,683, a reduction of $747. (See Chart 3.)

William and Laura Smith have been married two years, have

CHART 3

Form 1	Individual Wage Tax		1997

Your first name and initial (if joint return, also give spouse's name and initial) Last name			Your social security number
Frank Jones			234 56 7890
Home address (number and street including apartment number or rural route)			Spouse's social security number
1414 Elm St., Apt. 4			
City, town, or post office, state and ZIP code	Your occupation		Steelworker
Pittsburgh, PA	Spouse's occupation		

1 Wages and salary and Pensions	1		23,000
2 Personal allowance			
(a) $26,200 for married filing jointly	2(a)		
(b) $13,100 for single	2(b)		
(c) $17,200 for single head of household	2(c)		13,100
3 Number of dependents, not including spouse	3		0
4 Personal allowances for dependents *(line 3 multiplied by $5,300)*	4		0
5 Total personal allowances *(line 2 plus line 4)*	5		13,100
6 Taxable wages *(line 1 less line 5, if positive: otherwise zero)*	6		9,900
7 Tax *(17% of line 6)*	7		1,683
8 Tax already paid	8		
9 Tax due *(line 7 less line 8, if positive)*	9		
10 Refund due *(line 8 less line 7, if positive)*	10		

one child, and have a combined income of $30,000 (there is no marriage penalty under a flat tax, so the proportions of income earned by either do not matter). They are saving for a down payment but do not yet own a home and therefore do not find it profitable to itemize deductions. They saw a news report that said the rich are the only ones who will benefit from a flat tax. This causes them needless worry. Under the current tax system, they pay $2,273. Under a 17 percent flat tax, their income tax bill falls to zero. (See Chart 4.)

Andy and Jill Williams have three children, live in a home with a mortgage, give regularly to their church, and earn $60,000 per year. They worry that losing their deductions for their mortgage and charitable donations under a flat tax will hurt them. Not true. Under the current tax system, they pay $3,342. Under a 17 percent flat tax, their bill falls to $3,043, a reduction of $299. (See Chart 5.)

To figure out your tax bill under the flat tax, just use the simple postcard and see whether your tax bill goes up or down.

Filling out the postcard, however, only lets you know your

direct benefits from a flat tax. There are other benefits as well, ones that are less obvious, but no less real. We've already talked about the advantages of eliminating costly and time-consuming tax preparation. And as we have discussed, tax reform can boost economic growth, the engine of prosperity that makes it possible for higher wages and a higher standard of living.

A higher standard of living is also made possible by lower interest rates. By shifting the tax on interest income from the individual recipient to the payer, a flat tax will lower interest rates dramatically. The reason for this drop is that lenders would no longer be taxed on the interest they receive. As a result, the interest rate would not have to include a tax "premium" (much as interest rates fell under President Reagan when inflation was reduced—lenders could charge lower rates but still make money). Look at it this way. Right now you may be willing to "loan" the bank money at 5 percent, knowing that some of the interest you earn will go to the government in taxes. But if no taxes were being taken out, you

CHART 4

Form 1	Individual Wage Tax	1997

Your first name and initial (if joint return, also give spouse's name and initial)	Last name	Your social security number
William and Laura Smith		239	01	9513

Home address (number and street including apartment number or rural route)	Spouse's social security number
123 Main St.,	531	22	1704

City, town, or post office, state and ZIP code	Your occupation	Truck Driver
Middletown, OH	Spouse's occupation	Teacher's Aide

1	Wages and salary and Pensions	1	30,000
2	Personal allowance		
	(a) $26,200 for married filing jointly	2(a)	
	(b) $13,100 for single	2(b)	
	(c) $17,200 for single head of household	2(c)	26,200
3	Number of dependents, not including spouse	3	1
4	Personal allowances for dependents (line 3 multiplied by $5,300)	4	5,300
5	Total personal allowances (line 2 plus line 4)	5	31,500
6	Taxable wages (line 1 less line 5, if positive; otherwise zero)	6	0
7	Tax (17% of line 6)	7	0
8	Tax already paid	8	
9	Tax due (line 7 less line 8, if positive)	9	
10	Refund due (line 8 less line 7, if positive)	10	

CHART 5

Form 1	Individual Wage Tax		1997

Your first name and initial (If joint return, also give spouse's name and initial)   Last name

Andy   Jill   Williams

Your social security number

589 | 31 | 8501

Home address (number and street including apartment number or rural route)

1501 1st St.

Spouse's social security number

846 | 44 | 1552

City, town, or post office, state and ZIP code

Pleasantville, CA

Your occupation Manager

Spouse's occupation Homemaker

1	Wages and salary and Pensions	1	60,000
2	Personal allowance		
	(a) $26,200 for married filing jointly	2(a)	
	(b) $13,100 for single	2(b)	
	(c) $17,200 for single head of household	2(c)	26,200
3	Number of dependents, not including spouse	3	3
4	Personal allowances for dependents (line 3 multiplied by $5,300)	4	15,900
5	Total personal allowances (line 2 plus line 4)	5	42,100
6	Taxable wages (line 1 less line 5, if positive: otherwise zero)	6	17,900
7	Tax (17% of line 6)	7	3,043
8	Tax already paid	8	
9	Tax due (line 7 less line 8, if positive)	9	
10	Refund due (line 8 less line 7, if positive)	10	

might find it worthwhile to "loan" the bank your money even at 4 percent. An economist at the Federal Reserve Bank of Kansas City, for instance, estimates interest rates will fall by 25 to 35 percent. If interest rates are currently 8 percent, the rate under a flat tax would fall to 6 percent or below.

One of the worst casualties of the current tax system—trust—can't be understood just in terms of wages and interest rates or other numbers that fit easily into a cost-benefit analysis. The current tax system undermines our trust in elected officials. The Founding Fathers doubtless wanted citizens to have a healthy distrust of government, but the tax system encourages too many Americans to view the political process as hopelessly corrupt. With a flat tax, there is no opportunity for special-interest loopholes or other cozy deals for big campaign contributors. And there is no longer any justification for police-state tactics by the IRS. There would be less fear of government, and more trust as well.

CHAPTER 4
TODAY'S TAX SYSTEM:
ANTI-GROWTH AND ANTI-FAMILY

Today's tax code has few defenders. Nor are its critics limited to conservatives. House Minority Leader Richard Gephardt (D-Mo.) says of the current system:

> It has become a test of legal brainpower, an accountant's decathlon, a treasure hunt for hidden deductions and buried tax breaks. Our tax code has become a dense fog of incentives, inducements, and penalties that distort the most basic economic decisions, constrain the free market, and make it hard for Americans to run their own lives. The Internal Revenue Service has become a symbol of what is wrong with American government.

Or, as Senate Majority Leader Bob Dole (R-Kan.) summed it up:

> Tax policy has been a primary tool with which government has wielded power, fed the bureaucracy, and redistributed wealth.... Any fair system would not penalize, but instead reward people for working harder, investing wisely, and saving more. It would eliminate the lobbyist-drafted loopholes that benefit the few, but force the rest of us to pay.

The current income tax system not only hobbles the economy, it unfairly discriminates against taxpayers who work hard or lack special-interest protection. The tax code's problems, while seemingly endless, fall into several broad categories:

High tax rates—In today's convoluted tax system, a successful entrepreneur will pay more than forty cents of each additional dollar earned to the federal government. This burden can rise to more than fifty cents when state income taxes are included, and to more than eighty cents when federal death taxes are added. These excessive rates penalize working and saving. A people cannot be free when their government seizes such a large share of their income. Nor is this a problem limited to the so-called rich. According to the Tax Foundation, "Tax Freedom Day"—the day when an *average family* will have earned enough to pay its federal, state, and local taxes and can begin keeping money for food, clothing, and shelter—did not occur last year until May 6. (See Chart 6.)

Complexity—Today's tax system has more than six hundred forms for taxpayers. Most of us, of course, are lucky enough to avoid all but a few of these technical monstrosities. Even so, the average taxpayer is often subject to bewildering difficulties. Consider this: The simplest of all tax forms, the 1040EZ, requires thirty-one pages of instructions in fine print worthy of a used-car contract. Not surprisingly, more and more bewildered Americans pay professionals to fill out their tax forms. Even though only 29 percent of taxpayers itemize, fully 50 percent pay experts to do their tax returns. According to the Tax Foundation, annual compliance costs total nearly $200 billion simply for the time we spend, together with the bills for all the accountants, tax lawyers, and lobbyists we must pay to be on the safe side with the IRS.

Multiple taxation—Under the current system, the IRS gets to come back over and over again for another bite at the apple. Some forms of income, particularly from savings and investment, are sub-

CHART 6

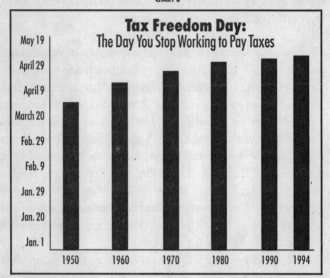

Tax Freedom Day:
The Day You Stop Working to Pay Taxes

ject to as many as four levels of tax. A single dollar of income, for example, could be hit by corporate income tax, personal income tax, capital gains tax, and estate taxes.

Social engineering—Manipulating the tax code has become lawmakers' favorite method for manipulating citizens. There are extra taxes to keep us from saving and investing and tax breaks to encourage us to do what Washington defines as the right things. Taxation should be about collecting revenue for the government so that it can do its job. Instead, taxes have become a tool for legislators to tell us how to live our lives. Simplifying the tax code takes away power that Washington has over our lives: It is one of the simplest steps we can take to restore our personal freedoms.

CHAPTER 5
REINING IN THE INTERNAL REVENUE SERVICE

By dramatically reducing the complexities of the current system, the flat tax would leave taxpayers with less reason to fear the IRS. For individual taxpayers, the only possible areas of controversy under a flat tax are the size of their family and the amount of labor income earned (taxes on capital income are withheld and paid at the business level). Whatever problems remain—for example, how the self-employed would handle business expenses—would be a fraction of those that exist now.

Many Washington insiders dismiss IRS problems by noting that the vast majority of taxpayers take the standard deduction and fill out simple 1040 tax returns. These insiders—most of whom hire experts to fill out *their* tax returns—might want to keep the following statistics in mind:

For many years, *Money* magazine conducted a test of professional tax preparers, a sort of contest to see who could most accurately file a hypothetical tax return. Almost invariably, the result was the same: None of the experts' answers was the same, and none was correct.

The IRS sent out 33 million penalty notices in 1993 demanding money for 140 different reasons. And who knows how accurate those demands are? In a devastating critique of the IRS in a Cato Institute paper, Daniel Pilla noted that about half of the 10 million correction notices sent out by the IRS each year are wrong. We are penalized if we make a mistake calculating our taxes, but not so the

IRS: According to Pilla, the IRS gives wrong answers to more than 8 million taxpayers a year who call to ask how to comply with the tax law.

Mistakes made by the IRS are not insubstantial. The government's own General Accounting Office (GAO) charges that the IRS has $200 billion of misstated payments and refunds on its books. This should come as little surprise given that the GAO found that the IRS couldn't even account for nearly two-thirds of its own budget.

Nonetheless, the IRS takes a dim, and unforgiving, view when others make mistakes. The absurd IRS penalty process fined one taxpayer $155.27 for underpaying his taxes by 1¢.

In a similar case, the IRS attempted to fine a company $46,806.37 for an alleged underpayment of 10¢.

Or how about the case of an IRS raid on a day-care center? Agents refused to release children until the parents signed papers agreeing to pay the government.

IRS employees have even been caught snooping in the tax returns of their neighbors, violating rights of privacy.

It isn't that the IRS is a rogue agency full of tax-collecting storm troopers out to trample citizens' rights. The real problem is that the tax law has become so arbitrary and incomprehensible that not even the government agents enforcing it can make heads or tails of it. As former IRS Commissioner Shirley Peterson testified before Congress, "Many taxpayers fail to comply because they cannot easily understand what they are supposed to do."

A flat tax will dramatically reduce the power of the IRS. In a system where the only information individuals are obligated to provide is their total income and the size of their family, much of the uncertainty and fear would disappear. And while most individuals thankfully never have to experience the even greater complexities of the corporate income tax, the flat tax would generate equally dramatic savings for business. The money businesses now spend on lawyers, accountants, and lobbyists would be freed up for higher wages and more investment, thus helping make America more competitive. The following is a brief list of some of the ways in which a flat tax will reduce IRS intrusion into our lives:

- Under current law, many taxpayers and businesses are forced to compute their taxes two different ways and then pay the government whichever figure is higher. With a flat tax, the rules are the same for everyone and complicated provisions like the alternative minimum tax disappear.

- Under current law, business income is taxed twice, at both the corporate level and the individual level. This is not only bad economic policy, it also grants the government too much power since it requires the IRS to keep track of all shareholders and monitor exactly how much dividend income they receive. With a flat tax, the income is taxed once, at the business level, so the IRS would have no reason to snoop into anyone's investments.

- Under current law, income used for savings is double taxed. As is the case with dividends, this requires the IRS to track and monitor interest payments. With a flat tax, there is no double taxation and the tax falls on the institution paying the interest rather than the individual receiving the interest.

- Under current law, the IRS forces individuals and businesses to keep track of all capital gains. This means they must tell the government what they own, when they bought it, how much it cost, what improvements they made to it, and when they sold it. With a flat tax individuals are free from divulging their assets. Businesses get a similarly simple approach. They deduct the cost of any assets at the time of purchase and include the receipts of any sale the year they are received.

● Under current law, businesses are forbidden from subtracting from revenues the full cost of most investments to determine taxable income. This not only punishes investment, it guarantees the horrible complexity that comes from calculating multiyear depreciation. For small businesses and any company that makes many different investments, this is a logistical nightmare. With a flat tax, all businesses receive the same simple treatment. They get to fully deduct the expense of new investment the year in which it is made.

● Under current law, American businesses attempting to compete overseas endure huge compliance costs. They have to both pay taxes to the country in which they are operating and file with the IRS. Since American companies couldn't compete if they had to pay full-fledged taxes in two countries, our government gives U.S. companies a credit for taxes paid to other governments. But since most governments have heavier taxes than the United States, the IRS collects very little money on American overseas business: The policy generates not revenue, but merely an absurd paperwork burden. With a flat tax, the U.S. government would tax businesses on income they earn in the United States and foreign governments would continue to tax businesses on income they earn overseas. It's that simple.

CHAPTER 6
CLEANING UP WASHINGTON CORRUPTION

There are 12,609 special interests officially registered to lobby in Washington, and the tax code is one of their chief targets. Retired members of Congress, former legislative staff members, consulting firm employees, and law firm partners are among those who can earn up to five hundred dollars an hour wielding influence in the tax-writing committees of Congress. This process has caused America's tax system, which began in 1913 with one simple form, to grow into today's monstrosity.

While lobbyists are very well compensated for their efforts (and not all of them are looking for special loopholes; some are just fighting to keep their tax bills from increasing), the biggest winners are the politicians. Chart 7 shows the average contribution levels for members of the House tax-writing committee compared with the average for other House members. If you write tax law, a lot of people want to give you money. A huge portion of the difference comes from PAC contributions—the special interests. (See Chart 8.) No wonder the House Ways and Means and Senate Finance Committees are considered the plum assignments.

The billions of dollars spent on lobbying and campaign contributions are a drain on the productive sector of the economy. Imagine if business were able to invest that money, not in chasing tax loopholes, but it creating jobs and building factories.

The original income tax started out simple enough, of course. What's to guarantee that a reformed and newly flattened tax won't

CHART 7

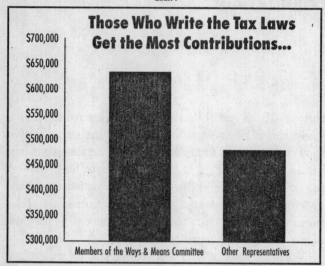

Those Who Write the Tax Laws Get the Most Contributions...

Members of the Ways & Means Committee	Other Representatives

just succumb to the pressures of special-interest groups in the future? What would happen if a very liberal Congress and president were elected down the road? Would the flat tax be undone? This fear, quite legitimate, is why a flat tax should be accompanied by a

CHART 8

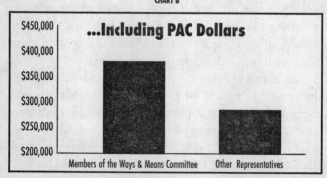

...Including PAC Dollars

Members of the Ways & Means Committee	Other Representatives

requirement that politicians obtain a two-thirds supermajority in both the House and Senate before any tax code changes are made.

While a supermajority is a good safety mechanism, it is probably one that will never be used. Once a flat tax is in place, it is unlikely that voters will ever allow politicians to go back to the old system. We know this from worldwide evidence. Hong Kong's effective 15 percent flat tax, for instance, has proven very stable (though it may not be able to withstand communism—Hong Kong will be turned over to China in 1997).

This is backed up by the experiences of various states. The commonwealth of Massachusetts has a flat tax, which the big spenders are always trying to destroy. As recently as 1994, they put a referendum on the ballot to turn the flat tax into a so-called progressive tax. The tax-and-spend crowd told voters it would only be the "rich" who would pay more, but the people figured that any change would be the camel's nose under the tent and everyone's taxes would go up sooner or later. When the votes were counted, the "liberal" voters of Massachusetts affirmed their support for a flat tax by a margin of 69 percent to 31 percent.

Even so, a supermajority provision would be a valuable shield against the fiscal irresponsibility of future politicians. Right now a number of states have supermajority provisions and they tend to have lower taxes and spending than other states.

CHAPTER 7
THE STATE-BY-STATE IMPACT

In addition to simplicity and faster growth, a properly designed flat tax also provides much-needed tax relief. As Chart 9 indicates, the benefits of the flat tax to individual taxpayers would be considerable. The benefits vary somewhat from state to state, but in every state the average household benefits a lot.

It is important to note that this chart shows only that average tax liabilities and the total tax bill will be reduced under a flat tax of 17 percent. Some taxpayers will see greater savings and others will see lesser savings. There will be a few—primarily those who

CHART 9

States That Benefit Most From a 17% Flat Tax

Average per Houshold Dollar Savings		Federal Tax Savings for All Taxpayers (in Billions)		% Reduction in Average Household Tax Bill	
Connecticut	$1,856	New York	$9.81	South Dakota	38.28%
New Jersey	1,521	Texas	8.03	North Dakota	32.63
Illinois	1,511	Illinois	8.00	Indiana	30.78
North Dakota	1,506	Florida	7.98	Florida	30.16
Virginia	1,463	Ohio	6.58	Rhode Island	30.02
Indiana	1,415	Pennsylvania	6.08	Missouri	29.45
Rhode Island	1,406	Michigan	5.77	Ohio	28.92
Washington	1,385	New Jersey	5.63	Iowa	28.86
Michigan	1,372	California	5.30	Maine	28.85
Florida	1,335	Virginia	4.09	Illinois	28.81

benefit from loopholes and other special tax breaks—who will wind up paying more in taxes.

Those states that already have flat taxes provide useful evidence of how a flat tax will work. The Joint Economic Committee recently published a report on state tax systems to find out whether the type of tax had any impact on the state's economic performance. Not surprisingly, states with flat taxes outperformed states with "progressive" tax rates. Personal income increased by a healthy 223 percent in flat-tax states over the last thirty years. States with tax systems that punished success by strapping taxpayers with graduated tax rates saw personal incomes rise by only 175 percent.

States with flat taxes are also, on average, more fiscally responsible. A report by the Alexis de Tocqueville Institution found that in the 1980s, flat-tax states increased inflation-adjusted spending by 19.7 percent. States with tax systems that penalized success, on the other hand, boosted spending by 31.8 percent. In flat-tax states, taxpayers are united in the knowledge that increased spending means higher taxes for everyone. In so-called progressive tax states, politicians are able to use class warfare—and the promise that someone else will be doing the paying—to divide and conquer their taxpayers.

CHAPTER 8
RENEWING THE AMERICAN
JOB CREATION MACHINE

During the 1980s, lower tax rates helped trigger an amazing 21 million new jobs and pushed family incomes to record highs. Unfortunately, tax increases during both the Bush and Clinton administrations have undermined the economy's subsequent performance, and job creation, economic growth, and incomes have been sluggish in recent years.

In a world where money reacts quickly to changes in a nation's business climate, a tax system that rewards entrepreneurship will attract increased investment and job creation. A system that penalizes growth with high tax rates and imposes multiple levels of taxation on capital income, by contrast, will drive investors and their dollars away. America has undermined its ability to compete by raising tax rates while most of our competitors have been cutting tax rates.

A flat tax will help reverse this worrisome trend by recognizing a fundamental truth too often ignored in Washington. Simply stated, employers are not charities and people are not fools. If the tax system raises the cost of creating jobs, businesses will be less likely to create them; if taxes are too high, individuals will be discouraged from working, saving, and investing.

Workers are paid by and large on the basis of what they produce. What they produce is determined by the quality and quantity of technology, machinery, expertise, plant, and equipment with which they work. This is why workers in the United States,

Germany, and Japan earn more than workers in Brazil, India, and Nigeria. When you produce more, you get paid more.

The tools that make workers more valuable come about through savings and investment. Taxes on savings and investment, however, reduce incentives to invest in tools and technology needed to make workers more productive.

Some may wish to dismiss this analysis as "trickle-down" economics, but even liberal economists admit that workers' wages depend on savings and investment. Every economic theory recognizes that the way to increase incomes is to make workers more productive by giving them more and better tools with which to produce. As liberal economist Paul Samuelson has written:

> What happens to the wage rate now that each person works with more capital goods? Because each worker has more capital to work with, his or her marginal product rises. Therefore, the competitive real wage rises as workers become worth more to capitalists and meet with spirited bidding up of their market wage rates.

Translated out of economists' jargon, he is saying that higher wages depend on savings and investment. Or consider the views of the Clinton White House. In the 1994 Economic Report of the President, the administration noted that:

> The reasons for wanting to raise the investment share of the GDP [gross domestic product] are straightforward: Workers are more productive when they are equipped with more and better capital, more productive workers earn higher real wages, and higher real wages are the mainspring of higher living standards. Few economic propositions are better supported than these— or more important.

The president may routinely ignore this advice, but his economists are right. If we want workers' wages to increase, or if we want new, high-paying jobs, we need to stimulate savings and investment. Unfortunately, many provisions of our tax code are seemingly designed to punish people who save and invest. Among the tax laws that hurt workers' wages are:

- *The capital gains tax*—Under current law, a worker earns money, then pays tax on the money. If the worker tries to build a nest egg by buying some stock, the government will tax him a second time on any increase in the value of his stock. To make a bad situation even worse, the IRS even taxes the portion of the gain that simply represents inflation. Under a flat tax, the capital gains tax is abolished.
- *The death tax*—In one of the clearest examples of double taxation, the government confiscates as much as 55 percent of people's assets when they die. This is money that was taxed when first earned. The politicians justify this tax on estates by claiming it only hits the rich. Many of the so-called rich, however, are small businesses and family farms that have to be broken up and sold to pay the tax. Breaking up businesses is hardly the way to create new and better-paying jobs.
- *Dividend double taxation*—When income is earned by a business, it is subject to the corporate income tax. That same income, however, is taxed a second time when distributed to shareholders (the owners of the business). The government should tax it at the business level or they should tax it at the individual level, but they should not be able to tax the same dollars two times. Under a flat tax, the double tax on dividends is abolished.

CHAPTER 9
ENDING THE POISON OF
CLASS WARFARE

Some dismiss the flat tax as a free ride for the rich. Actually, under a flat tax, the rich do not get a free ride: They pay substantially more than the poor. A wealthy taxpayer with one hundred times more taxable income than his neighbor will pay one hundred times more in taxes, with no loopholes to hide in.

Indeed, the liberals who think the flat tax is only for the rich should be among its biggest supporters. Consider the following features of the flat tax with which honest liberals should agree:

- The key philosophical principle of the flat tax is equality. All taxpayers play by the same rules, no matter how wealthy they are. The elimination of loopholes, preferences, credits, exclusions, subsidies, and deductions should be particularly attractive to honest people of all ideologies who want the government to apply the laws equally.
- If the rich are able to shield their income with shelters and preferences, the tax burden falls disproportionately on lower- and middle-income workers. Eliminating loopholes allows for lower taxes for those with lower incomes.
- Because of a generous family-based allowance, the poor are shielded from the income tax burden. A family of four under the Armey-Shelby flat tax pays no income tax on their first $33,300.
- Lower-income and middle-income taxpayers will enjoy a more financially secure retirement if they are not forced to pay a double tax on their savings.

Class warfare has long been a rallying cry for the liberal troops. But the flat tax is no valentine to the rich, even judged by liberals' own criteria. The experience of three decades—the 1920s, the 1960s, and the 1980s—shows how the rich pay more when marginal tax rates are reduced.

In the 1920s, tax rates were reduced from a high of 73 percent to 25 percent between 1921 and 1926. Did the rich get a free ride? Hardly: The share of the tax burden paid by those making more than $50,000—a great deal of money back then—rose dramatically, climbing from 44.2 percent in 1921 to 78.4 percent in 1928.

In the 1960s, the Kennedy tax cuts lowered the top rate from 91 percent to 70 percent. The result: Tax collections from those making more than $50,000 per year climbed by 57 percent between 1963 and 1966, while tax collections from those earning below $50,000 rose 11 percent. As a result, the rich saw their portion of the income tax burden climb from 11.6 percent to 15.1 percent.

In the 1980s, Ronald Reagan reduced the top rate from 70 percent in 1980 to 28 percent in 1988. The share of income taxes paid by the top 10 percent of earners jumped significantly, climbing from 48 percent in 1981 to 57 percent in 1988.

In each of these decades, lowering tax rates removed incentives to hide income, shelter income, reduce earnings, and transfer money overseas. The result: Upper-income taxpayers were willing to earn and report more taxable income, and the amount of tax they paid increased. The evidence speaks for itself.

Chart 10 illustrates how the three best-known deductions offer almost no benefit to the poor and middle class. Upper-income and wealthy taxpayers, by contrast, benefit immensely. And while the flat tax eliminates tax shelters that help the rich, there will remain one loophole, a personal exemption that protects the poor. Under the Armey-Shelby proposal (H.R. 2060, S. 1050), a family of four would pay no tax on its first $33,300 in income. Every dollar over $33,300 would be taxed at the same low 17 percent rate. This personal allowance, which is indexed to inflation to prevent bracket creep, is considerably above the poverty level and will ensure that even the low rate of a flat tax is not an impediment to those trying to climb the economic ladder.

As Chart 11 illustrates, the personal allowance also has the effect of making the tax system progressive. Since no earnings are taxed until after the $33,300 mark has been reached, the tax rate on a family of four with $30,000 of income would be zero. A family with $40,000 in income would pay 17 percent of the amount over $33,300, or 17 percent of $6,700. That family's overall effective rate is 2.8 percent. That figure rises to 5.7 percent for a family with earn-

CHART 10

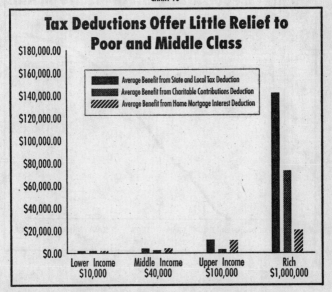

ings of $50,000. The effective rate continues to rise with income, reaching 9.5 percent on $75,000 of income, 11.3 percent on $100,000 of income, and 14.2 percent on $200,000 of income. For the well-to-do, the effective rate approaches 17 percent, as families with $500,000 of income pay 15.9 percent and a millionaire's household would pay 16.4 percent

The flat tax is a particularly important test for liberals. They must decide which is more important: maintaining lobbying power in Washington and keeping a tax system that satisfies an ideological impulse to punish success or adopting a system that ends special-interest corruption and helps boost the living standards of the less fortunate.

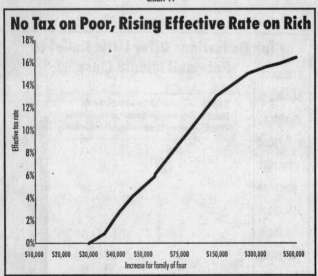

CHART 11

No Tax on Poor, Rising Effective Rate on Rich

CHAPTER 10
THE FLAT TAX AND THE DEFICIT

Another frequent attack against the flat tax is that it will increase the deficit. At first blush the criticism might appear sound. After all, most taxpayers will pay less.

This approach, however, assumes that the growth of the economy and the rate of government spending are locked in concrete. Using this simplistic approach, it is mathematically easy to estimate the impact of a flat tax on the deficit. If the flat tax rate is set at a high level, it will collect more money for the government; at a low level, it will collect less money for the government; and of course there is a flat tax rate that will collect the same amount of money as the current system. If the economy and government spending continue on their same path, opponents are right: The 17 percent flat tax sponsored by Majority Leader Armey will collect less money than the current system.

These assumptions about spending and the economy are dead wrong.

For starters, opponents conveniently overlook the fact that the Armey flat tax specifically calls for strict controls on government spending. These spending provisions include limits on both overall spending growth and a mechanism to bring entitlement spending under control. This portion of the bill ensures that the flat tax will not increase the deficit in the long run, even if it were the case that a flat tax would bring in less money than today's convoluted system.

There is, however, a final piece to the puzzle. When the economy grows faster, tax revenues grow as well—even under lower rates. Companies that earn more money, after all, pay higher taxes. Every new job created also creates a new taxpayer. To estimate the deficit impact of a flat tax one has to factor in the revenues that will come into the Treasury if the economy grows faster.

When opponents of the flat tax claim the deficit will be higher, they are usually forgetting to include the impact of the spending reductions, and they are always neglecting to factor in the impact of taxes on growth. Flat-tax critics generally assume that taxes have no impact on the economy. This is a common and venerable mistake made even by the government's official economic experts.

The experts should know better—and have in the past. Andrew Mellon, Treasury secretary during the 1920s, showed a great understanding of tax policy when he wrote: "The history of taxation shows that taxes which are inherently excessive are not paid. The high rates inevitably put pressure upon the taxpayer to withdraw his capital from productive business and invest it in tax-exempt securities or to find other lawful methods of avoiding the realization of taxable income. The result is that the sources of taxation are drying up; wealth is failing to carry its share of the tax burden; and capital is being diverted into channels which yield neither revenue to the Government nor profit to the people."

To be fair, the professional revenue estimators at the Joint Committee on Taxation (JCT) understand that "static" revenue estimates are unrealistic. In the past, however, liberal JCT chairmen like Chicago's Dan Rostenkowski were able to dictate that the JCT use methods that justified higher taxes. After the 1994 elections, however, Representative Bill Archer of Texas took over as chairman of the JCT; he already has directed the staff to update and modernize the revenue-estimating process.

Congress's JCT is not the only source of revenue estimates in Washington. It will come as no surprise that most of the attack numbers against the flat tax have come from the heavily politicized Clinton Treasury Department. The White House has made three separate estimates of the tax rate that would be needed for the flat tax to collect the same amount of money as the current tax system (remember, these numbers do not count the spending cuts and they also assume that the economy will stay exactly the same). The first time, they projected that the rate would have to be 25.8 percent. The second projection was that the rate would have to be 22.9 percent. The latest estimate now shows that the rate would have to be 20.8 percent.

But these estimates fail to recognize that people change their behavior when the law changes—that tax policy affects what people do with their money. You would think that Washington would have figured it out by now, given the wealth of painful experiences when taxes have been raised. President Herbert Hoover's decision to hike tax rates from 25 percent to 63 percent (and you thought Clinton was bad) resulted in tax revenues falling rather than rising. And tax revenues were nearly flat during the Eisenhower years, as a top tax rate of 91 percent discouraged productive behavior.

More recently, consider the steep luxury tax on yachts passed by Congress in 1990. Rich people were able to avoid paying the tax simply by refusing to buy yachts, or by purchasing their craft overseas. The only impact of the legislation was to bankrupt many American shipbuilders and throw their workers into the unemployment lines. Instead of collecting money with the luxury tax on yachts, the government actually lost money as shipbuilders and their workers lost their livelihoods.

In 1993, the Clinton administration proposed the biggest income tax rate increase since Herbert Hoover. This rate increase was projected to boost tax collections by more than $100 billion over five years. The evidence is already showing, however, that income tax collections have been stagnant. Why? It turns out that upper-income taxpayers are not stupid. When the government punishes them for working, saving, investing, and taking risks, they respond accordingly. They cut back on their hours, put their money in tax shelters, hide their assets overseas, and take other steps to protect their earnings. Since these are the people who are most able to afford the services of tax lawyers, accountants, and lobbyists, it should come as no surprise that tax increases designed to "soak the rich" are total failures.

Today's lawmakers would be well advised to listen to the words of President John F. Kennedy: "Our true choice is not between tax reduction, on the one hand, and the avoidance of large Federal deficits on the other. It is increasingly clear that no matter what party is in power, so long as our national security needs keep rising, an economy hampered by restrictive tax rates will never produce enough revenues to balance our budget just as it will never produce enough jobs or enough profits," Kennedy said. "The soundest way to raise the revenues in the long run is to cut the rates now."

CHAPTER 11
A COMPREHENSIVE PLAN
FOR BALANCING THE BUDGET

Ultimately the flat tax will require a strategy for balancing the budget. Ronald Reagan's tax cuts in the 1980s, as we have seen, actually dramatically increased tax revenues to the Treasury. But liberals in Congress persisted in going on a spending bender, hemorrhaging money even faster than it came in. The result? Skyrocketing deficits. And even though these deficits were the fault of excessive spending, it has been all too easy for liberals to blame the Reagan tax cuts. This fairy tale provides liberals with their justification for repeated efforts to undo Reagan's achievement, efforts that finally came to fruition with Bill Clinton's 1993 tax hike. Even if a flat tax produces greater revenues for the Treasury—as it very well might—the success of the reformed tax system could be discredited if deficits soar. To ensure the success of fundamental tax reform, we need to ensure that federal spending is reined in. Federalism provides the answer.

The goal of federalism is to give back to the states powers and responsibilities that were snatched by the federal government in the last sixty-five years. When federal programs are shut down and the job is handed back to the states, federal spending could be drastically reduced. Paying for locally controlled programs should rest with states and localities. Then decisions about when and how much to tax, and when and how much to spend, will be considered together, and considered at the state and local level, where citizens can have much more direct participation.

Federalism, like the flat tax, is a tremendously popular concept, but some members of Congress will be reluctant to tackle programs. Another problem is that state and local lawmakers, constrained by balanced budget requirements, are extremely concerned that any widespread elimination of federal programs would force them to raise taxes or reduce services in order to fulfill their newfound responsibilities. These concerns could be alleviated if sponsors of the flat tax lower the federal tax even further, as Congressman Armey has done, to make the plan as attractive as possible by protecting taxpayers against any increase in their combined federal, state, and local tax bill.

Linking the flat tax and federalism may kill two birds with one stone in theory, but will it work in reality? After all, in order to unequivocally guarantee that a flat tax would be a net tax cut for every income class and industry, the rate would have to be a couple of points below 20 percent. The numbers say yes. According to the administration's budget, outlays for grant programs in 1995 totaled more than $228 billion (this does not include the many government programs directly administered by the federal government and easily transferable to state and local control). And since the JCT estimates that each percentage point reduction in the flat tax rate "costs" the government around $35 billion per year, it is readily apparent that a deficit-neutral flat tax of 15 percent or less is easily achievable.

A comprehensive government reform package combining sweeping tax reform and program devolution creates an ideal political dynamic in which the appeal of the whole is greater than the appeal of the two parts considered separately. For lawmakers seeking a positive, pro-growth agenda heading into 1996 and beyond, joining the flat tax with a thorough-going federalism is just the ticket.

CHAPTER 12
RATING OTHER TAX REFORM PLANS

Tax reform is gaining momentum. The Armey-Shelby flat tax is the most popular and most widely known of the proposed reforms, and it certainly would solve the many problems of the current system, but there are other plans. Another extensively discussed option has been a proposal to replace the income tax with a national sales tax. In addition, there are a number of plans that would leave the basic structure of the existing system in place while making changes to certain components.

While there is widespread agreement on what is wrong with the tax system, there is considerable debate over which plan most completely solves these problems. The question is, which approach would be best for taxpayers and the economy? The following are the key features of the two other major approaches to tax reform currently under consideration:

National retail sales tax—This proposal would replace the personal and corporate income taxes with a tax on economic transactions. Many details remain unknown, such as what tax rate would be applied and what goods and services, if any, would be exempted. Under a national sales tax, the money is collected when a consumer makes a final purchase.

The fine tuning approaches—Several plans fit into this category. House Minority Leader Richard Gephardt has a plan that broadens the tax base by eliminating such preferences as deductions for charitable contributions and state and local taxes. He also would tax the value of fringe benefits, and his plan replaces the five tax brackets in the current system with five new brackets ranging between 10 percent and 34 percent.

Another plan has been offered by Senators Nunn and Domenici. Called the *USA tax*, their bill creates the equivalent of an unlimited individual retirement account (IRA) and replaces the current rate structure with a three-rate system that includes a top rate of 40 percent. Some deductions are lost or curtailed, and at least one new deduction is created. The corporate income tax would be replaced by a value-added tax (explained below).

To determine how these plans compare to a flat tax, it is necessary to see how well they satisfy the principles of a well-designed tax system. These are the key benchmarks by which all tax plans should be judged and how the major competitors to a flat tax fare:

- *Single low rate*—The sales-tax approach scores highly since supporters have stated they want a single low rate.

  The fine tuning approaches, both Gephardt's and the USA tax, receive low grades because they keep multiple tax rates and therefore do not treat citizens equally.
- *Simplicity*—The sales-tax approach scores highly since this system, properly designed, would eliminate most of the compliance costs of the current system.

  The fine tuning approaches do not score as well since they retain many deductions and often do not address the problems faced by business.
- *Savings and investment*—The sales-tax approach again scores highly because this type of system removes the bias in the existing system against savings and investment.

The fine tuning approaches have mixed grades. The Gephardt plan actually exacerbates the bias by increasing the amount of income that is double taxed. By contrast, the USA proposal largely eliminates the problem by creating an unlimited IRA.

● *Fairness*—The sales-tax approach scores highly in one sense since all taxpayers will pay the same rate, and all goods and services will be taxed.

The fine tuning approaches are mediocre. They retain deductions and keep tax rates that discriminate against citizens on the basis of their income.

Judged by the key principles of a fair, pro-growth tax system, the sales-tax approach is in many ways just as desirable as the flat tax. In the final analysis, however, the theoretical attributes of a sales tax begin to erode when confronted with several intractable problems. Unless sales-tax supporters can overcome the following obstacles, they should join forces with flat-tax fans to topple the existing system:

1. *The sales tax would require repeal of the Sixteenth Amendment, a virtually impossible undertaking.* Perhaps the biggest advantage of the flat tax over the sales tax is that there is no need to change the Constitution. By contrast, any legitimate effort to impose a sales tax must be joined with a repeal of the amendment that gives the government the power to levy an income tax. That, of course, is a daunting task. A constitutional amendment requires approval by two-thirds of both chambers of Congress and then must get the further blessing of thirty-eight state legislatures. The process is so grueling that even extremely popular constitutional amendments, such as

the proposed amendment requiring a balanced budget, have faltered. The chances of changing the Constitution as part of a tax reform effort are virtually nil.

Some sales-tax supporters argue that an amendment is not necessary. They argue that we can trust politicians to repeal the income tax with legislation once a sales tax is in place. Unfortunately, there is absolutely no evidence that this would be a wise bet. Country after country in Europe has imposed direct consumption taxes accompanied by promises that some other tax would be eliminated or reduced. When the dust settled, however, the other original taxes always remained and the politicians wound up with a huge new source of tax revenue. All this new bureaucratic booty, to no one's surprise, was used to finance higher levels of spending.

There is not a single country, state, province, or other political jurisdiction anywhere in the world that has actually *replaced* an income-based tax with a consumption-based tax, rather than just ending up with both. Supporters of the sales tax are playing with fire and could wind up *raising* the burden on American taxpayers, as the sales tax did on European taxpayers.

2. *The sales tax would become a value-added tax (VAT), a hidden money machine for big spenders.* Supporters of a national sales tax highlight the differences between their proposal and a VAT, and they have good reason to. While economically identical to a sales tax, the VAT has the undesirable feature (to taxpayers, but not to government) of being hidden: Since the tax is collected at each stage of the production process, the cost of the tax is built into the price of goods. Consumers wind up paying a lot more for products, but they are unable to recognize

that government is to blame. Politicians in countries with VATs have found that they are very easy to raise.

Supporters of a national sales tax recognize this problem and should be commended for trying to ensure that the sales tax would be visible—that is, like a city sales tax, added to the price of a product at the cash register. But however well-intentioned, the sales-tax supporters are fighting against the tide of history. Most countries with VATs originally had some sort of retail sales tax. The sales taxes evolved into VATs because governments find VATs much more profitable.

3. *The sales tax is politically unpopular.* The proposal has fared miserably in national polls, with support rarely climbing above 20 percent and opponents outnumbering supporters by at least two to one.

In conclusion, there is one shot—and one shot only—to repeal our unfair, anti-growth tax system and replace it with something that boosts the economy and treats all taxpayers equally. Only one proposal, the flat tax, has the level of support and depth of backing to survive the difficult battle ahead. If taxpayers are divided among competing proposals, the forces of big government will probably have enough strength to preserve the status quo. Unifying in support of a flat tax is the surest strategy for fundamental tax reform.

CHAPTER 13
WHY HOME OWNERS WIN BIG

The biggest scare tactic levied against the flat tax has been the claim that eliminating deductions for home mortgages will force middle-income taxes to rise while crashing the real estate market. The argument goes like this: If mortgages are no longer valuable for tax purposes, the value of houses is diminished, and prices in the housing market will plummet. For those who already have houses and mortgages, this is a frightening scenario indeed.

But the fear is misplaced. The economy can't grow without the value of assets rising as well. When the economy is strong and incomes rise, consumers spend more on almost all goods and services. As a major component of family budgets, housing clearly follows this pattern. Projecting the exact value of housing in the future involves a greater level of uncertainty, but an analysis conducted by The Heritage Foundation estimated that an explosion in economic growth would boost home values between 7 percent and 14 percent in the five years following enactment of a flat tax.

So why are there so many accusations that home values will fall or that the housing industry will suffer? The answer can be found in the ways Washington interest groups manipulate policy and fabricate numbers to pursue their narrow agendas.

As talk of tax reform began to sweep the nation, the National Association of Realtors hired a for-profit consulting company to prepare a critical analysis of the flat tax. Not surprisingly, the results of the "study" were negative, predicting that enactment of a tax system that treats all taxpayers and all income equally would cause housing values to fall by 15 percent. The Realtors' study contains astonishing flaws, however, and falls apart under unbiased economic scrutiny.

The study was conducted by an organization—Data Resources Inc./McGraw Hill, or DRI—that has been accused of tailoring its results to whatever the client wants. This seedy practice was reported in a book about the 1986 Tax Reform Act, a book aptly titled *Showdown at Gucci Gulch*. During that debate, a potential client asked a DRI representative "What do you think you'll find?" The DRI representative responded by stating, "I don't have a contract with you or a check from you." After receiving a commitment for money, the DRI person asked, "What do you want us to find?" No ones knows for sure the deal struck by the DRI and the realtors Washington lobby, but the study DRI did on the flat tax has no credibility.

Understanding from the outset that its job was to attack the flat tax, DRI had to make several assumptions, some dishonest, others just bizarre, to generate the desired result. For instance:

1. DRI analyzed a flat tax with an initial rate of 25 percent, gradually phasing down to 21 percent. None of the existing flat-tax proposals include these rates. Of course there is a big difference in the results from a 25 percent rate and a 17 percent rate!

2. DRI did not properly estimate the drop in interest rates under a flat tax. According to the Kansas City Federal Reserve Bank, interest rates will drop by 25 percent to 35 percent. Other experts have similar estimates, but DRI deliberately underestimated the drop in mortgage rates. That's important because falling mortgage rates keep housing values *up* because more people can afford to buy houses.

3. DRI overestimated by as much as 30 percent the average marginal tax rate that applies to homeowners, thus overstating the tax benefits of the deduction.
4. The DRI economists assume that financial assets would lose value under a flat tax. Just the opposite is true, say most economists, and common sense. Lower taxes on savings and investment will boost the value of financial assets by increasing the after-tax income they produce.
5. DRI also failed to include in their assessment the effect on home values that will arise from higher incomes, even though their own study admitted that the flat tax would increase economic growth.

The flat tax represents a threat to the rich and powerful vested interests in Washington, D.C. To preserve special tax breaks, these interest groups peddle dishonest information to citizens. As cited above, however, the historical evidence strongly argues that a flat tax will be a bonanza for homeowners. Perhaps this is why polls of homeowners and realtors—actual realtors, not Washington lobbyists—find strong support for the flat tax.

And remember: Nations such as Ireland, Britain, Australia, Israel, Japan, and Canada all have home ownership rates equal to or greater than the United States, but *none of them has a home mortgage interest deduction.*

CHAPTER 14
GOOD TIMES AHEAD FOR CHARITIES

Another controversial topic in the tax reform debate is the impact on charities. Some in the nonprofit sector fear that private giving will dry up if the tax deduction for charitable contributions is eliminated. However understandable, this concern is misplaced. Economic evidence, particularly from the 1980s, indicates that charitable giving depends much more on changes in personal income than on the tax deduction for charitable contributions. In other words:

● When people make more money they give more to charity.
● But a change in the tax deduction does not affect giving very much.

Since a flat tax would cause the economy to grow and incomes to rise, it will almost certainly mean Americans will give *more* to charity.

Chart 12 illustrates the point. Chart 12 demonstrates that individual giving is closely tied to changes in personal income. Whether tax rates are rising or falling, the generosity of Americans depends on how much they have to give. On the other hand, there is no observable link between giving and the value of the associated tax deduction. If anything, the data show just the opposite: contributions rise when tax rates (and thus the value of the deduction) fall.

A flat tax with no deductions might cause some wealthy taxpayers to reduce their giving, but overall contributions would rise as the nation prospered. Moreover, fewer than one out of every four taxpayers (largely the rich) use the charitable contributions deduction. So most Americans who give to church and charity are not affected in any way by the deduction and would not even notice its elimination.

CHART 12

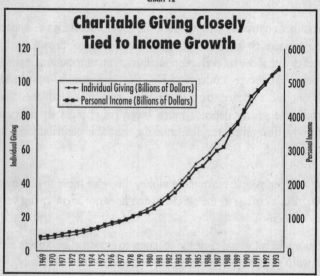

Charitable Giving Closely Tied to Income Growth

- Individual Giving (Billions of Dollars)
- Personal Income (Billions of Dollars)

CHAPTER 15
HOW THE FLAT TAX CAN HELP SENIORS NOW AND SAVE SOCIAL SECURITY

America's Social Security system is in deep trouble. The bipartisan entitlement commission estimates the system's unfunded liability (the differences between how much is promised and how much money will actually be available) at a staggering $7.3 trillion. With the baby boom generation approaching retirement, the Social Security Administration projects that the system will begin to run a deficit in less than fifteen years.

Some politicians tell us not to worry because the Trust Fund will have trillions of dollars accumulated with which to pay retirement benefits for the baby boom. Don't hold your breath; what the politicians neglect to tell you is that the so-called Trust Fund is full of nothing but IOUs. The surplus Social Security revenues have been being skimmed off and spent on other government programs. As a result, when retirement benefits begin to exceed Social Security tax collections in about fifteen years, the Trust Fund will be worthless.

The government will attempt to honor these IOUs, to be sure, but this can only be done by raising taxes, cutting spending, or issuing new debt. Pressure will quickly build to scale back promised benefits and/or raise Social Security taxes even more. Combined with a Medicare system that is teetering on the edge of insolvency (even the Republican rescue package would only avert Medicare's bankruptcy until about 2009), those who expect to be retired after the year 2010 face a perilous financial future.

This group includes, it should be noted, many of today's senior citizens.

The flat tax cannot save Social Security, but it will delay the system's ultimate collapse and create a way for today's workers to protect themselves from the coming catastrophe. In the short run, the flat tax will help by increasing the number of jobs and boosting incomes. Both of these developments will increase the amount of payroll taxes flowing into Social Security and should help keep the system solvent for a few extra years.

Even with increased payroll tax collections caused by higher growth, the Social Security system still will be unable to pay all promised benefits. The baby boomers, and those who come after them, will have to save a lot more of their own money to be able to retire in comfort. The current tax system, however, punishes those who save and invest by imposing double, triple, and even quadruple taxation of savings and investment income. Even if income is "only" double taxed, the dolorous effect on savings is dramatic.

The flat tax can help people begin to save for themselves. Chart 13 shows the difference in the nest eggs of someone who saves one thousand dollars a year under the current system and someone who saves the same amount in a flat-tax world in which income is taxed just once. As shown, the double tax on interest income imposed by today's tax code dramatically reduces the size of a retirement nest egg. By taxing income only once, the flat tax would allow interest earnings to compound, resulting in a nest egg almost twice as large than the same amount of savings would generate under current law.

If politicians fail to save Social Security, they will be condemning millions of Americans to unnecessary hardship. But why trust them to do the right thing? The flat tax can *almost* double our ability to protect ourselves.

CHART 13

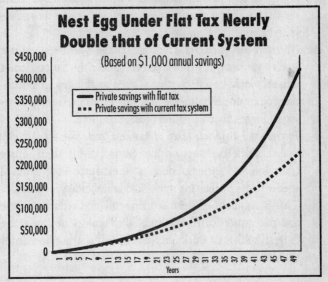

Nest Egg Under Flat Tax Nearly Double that of Current System

(Based on $1,000 annual savings)

— Private savings with flat tax
■ ■ ■ Private savings with current tax system

Years

The flat tax would be great for the entire country but *senior citizens would be among the biggest winners.* Consider the following:

● **No taxation of Social Security benefits.** One of the key principles of a flat tax is no double *taxation of savings.* This means either the money put into savings is deducted from that year's income and taxed when taken out (the IRA method) or the income is taxed when first earned but not subject to additional layers of tax on either principle or interest when ultimately consumed (the treatment received by municipal bonds). Armey and Shelby have chosen the "municipal bond" approach, so there is no deduction for payroll taxes. But there is no tax on Social Security benefits.

● **No capital gains tax.** As one of the most glaring examples of double taxation, the capital gains tax would be abolished under the flat tax. That is great for the elderly, who are far more likely to have capital gains than any other age group.

- *No estate and gift taxes.* These are double taxes because these assets were taxed when first earned. Under the flat tax, senior citizens would be able to pass on assets to children, grandchildren, or anyone else they see fit without the government coming in for yet another pound of flesh.

- *Interest and dividends taxed at business level.* The flat tax does not eliminate the taxes on interest and dividends, it simply taxes business earnings once at the source—the business itself—rather than taxing stock- and bondholders individually. That is far more efficient economically and reduces trouble and paperwork for all involved. Since seniors are by far the biggest holders of stocks and bonds, this is a big benefit for them.

The flat tax, based on the principle that all taxpayers and all income should be treated equally, would be good news for all taxpayers and great news for seniors.

CONCLUSION

The current income tax system punishes the economy, imposes heavy compliance costs on taxpayers, rewards special interests, and makes America less competitive. A flat tax would reduce these ill effects dramatically. Perhaps more importantly, it would reduce the federal government's power over the lives of taxpayers and get it out of the business of trying to micromanage the economy. There never will be a tax that is good for the economy, but the flat tax moves the system much closer to where it should be—raising the revenues government demands, but in the least destructive and least intrusive way possible

The one question this book has not answered, however, is how to achieve a flat tax. Politicians wield a lot of power and get a lot of campaign dollars as a result of the current tax code. Why would they ever do away with the source of their power, particularly those members who sit on the tax committees? The answer, of course, is that they will not relinquish that power unless the voters demand it. Ultimately, it is the people who will decide whether we have a tax system that reflects our highest values of equality and opportunity.

Please Join The Heritage Foundation

For only $15 you can become a member of the most influential conservative think tank in America. You'll receive a quarterly newsletter, a handsome membership card, and surveys that tell Congress what you think on important issues facing America. Your contribution will help Heritage's fight for a fair flat tax, smaller government and a growing economy.

Or Join Heritage's CongressWatchers

For your $100 contribution you become a member of the Heritage CongressWatchers. You'll receive free Heritage publications every month on the most important issues facing Congress, in addition to all the benefits of Heritage membership.

———————————————————————————

THE HERITAGE FOUNDATION
214 Massachusetts Ave., N.E.
Washington, DC 20002

☐ Yes. I want to become a member of The Heritage Foundation and help in the fight for a fair flat tax, smaller government and a growing economy.

I've chosen the following membership option:

☐ $15 membership fee

☐ $100 to join the Heritage CongressWatchers Club Please send me your latest selection of reports.

Enclosed is my check for $_____

Name_____

Address_____

City_____St._____Zip_____

BIG DISCOUNTS ON EXTRA COPIES
Please help spread the word about "The Flat Tax"

This concise book is packed with facts about how the "flat tax" will cut taxes, shrink spending, reduce the power of special interests, rein in the IRS, ignite the economy, and make government accountable.

Please consider ordering extra copies at bulk copy prices for friends, business and social associations, local political groups, radio talk show hosts, and newspaper editors.